WHAT *IS* POETRY?

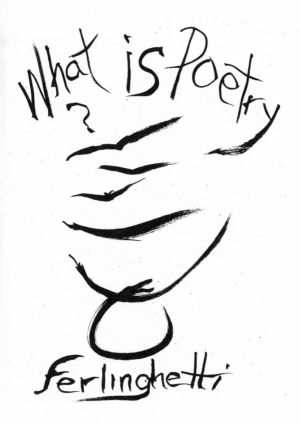

What is Poetry?

ferlinghetti

A Donald S. Ellis Book

CREATIVE ARTS BOOK COMPANY ✣ BERKELEY CALIFORNIA

For information contact:
Creative Arts Book Company
833 Bancroft Way
Berkeley, California 94710

ISBN 0-88739-369-1
Library of Congress Catalog Number 00-104557

Printed in the United States of America

NOTE

A very early prose version of this text was transcribed
from a KPFA (FM) broadcast recorded by the author in
the late 1950s under the title, *The Street's Kiss*.
It was published by the Limberlost Press (Boise, Idaho) in
1998. A later prose version was published in the author's
"Poetry As News" column in the San Francisco Chronicle
in 1999. The present edition is
much changed and enlarged.

WHAT *IS* POETRY?

Poetry is news
from the frontiers
of consciousness

Poetry is what we would cry out
upon awaking in a dark wood
in the middle of the journey
of our life

A poem is a mirror
walking down a high street
full of visual delight

Poetry is
the shook foil of the imagination
It should shine out
and half blind you

It is the sun streaming down
in the meshes of morning

It is white nights
and mouths of desire

It is made
by dissolving halos
in oceans of sound

It is the street talk
of angels and devils

It is a sofa full of blind singers
who have put aside their canes

A poem should arise to ecstasy
somewhere between speech and song

———————————————

A poem must sing
and fly away with you
or it's a dead duck
with a prose soul

Poetry is the anarchy of the senses
making sense

Poetry is all things born with wings
that sing

Like a bowl of roses
A poem should not have to be
explained

Poetry is a voice of dissent
against the waste of words
and the mad plethora of print

It is what exists
between the lines

It is made
with the syllables of dreams

It is far far cries
upon a beach at nightfall

It is a lighthouse
moving its megaphone
over the sea

It is a picture of Ma in her
Woolworth bra
looking out a window
into a secret garden

It is an Arab carrying
colored rugs and birdcages
through the streets
& a great metropolis

A poem can be made
of common household ingredients
It fits on a single page
yet it can fill a world
and fits in the pocket of a heart

The poet is a street singer
who rescues the alleycats of love

Poetry is pillow-thought
after intercourse

It is the distillation of articulate animals
calling to each other
across a great gulf

It is a pulsing fragment
of the inner life
an untethered music

It is the dialogue
of naked statues

It is the sound of summer in the rain
and of people laughing behind
closed shutters
down an alley at night

It is a bare lightbulb
in a homeless hotel
illuminating a nakedness
of minds and hearts

Let the poet be a singing animal
turned pimp
for an anarchist king

Poetry is
the incomparable lyric intelligence
brought to bear upon
fiftyseven varieties of experiece

Poetry is a high house echoing
with all the voices
that ever said anything crazy
or wonderful

Poetry is a subversive raid
upon the forgotten language
of the collective unconscious

Poetry is a real canary in a coal mine
and we know why the caged bird sings

Poetry is the shadow cast
by our streetlight imaginations

It is the voice
of the Fourth Person Singular

It is the voice
within the voice of the turtle

It is the face
behind the face of the race

Poetry is made of night-thoughts
If it can tear itself away from illusion
it will not be disowned
before the dawn

Poetry is made by evaporating
the liquid laughter of youth

Poetry is a book of light at night
dispersing clouds of unknowing

It hears the whisper
of elephants
and sees how many angels dance
on the head of a pin

It is a humming a keening
a laughing a sighing at dawn
a wild soft laughter

It is the final gestalt
of the imagination

Poetry should be emotion
recollected in emotion

Words are living fossils
The poet should
piece the wild beast together
and make it sing

A poet is only as great as his ear
Too bad if it is tin

Poetry is perpetual revolt
against silence exile and cunning

The poet a subversive barbarian
at the city gates
constantly challenging
our status quo

He is the master ontologist
constantly questioning reality
and reinventing it

He mixes drinks
out of the insane liquors
of the imagination
and is perpetually surprised
that no one staggers

He should be a dark barker
before the tents of existence

Poetry is what can be heard at manholes
echoing up Dante's fire escape

Poetry is religion
Religion is poetry

It is the humming of moths
as they circle the flame

It is a wood boat moored in the shade
under a weeping willow
in the bend of a river

_____

The poet must have wide-angle vision
each look a world glance
and the concrete is most poetic

Poetry is
not all heroin horses and Rimbaud
It is also the powerless prayers
of airline passengers
fastening their seatbelts
for the final descent

Poetry is the real subject
of great prose

It speaks the unspeakable
It utters the inutterable
sigh of the heart

Each poem a momentary madness
and the unreal is realist

A poem should still be
an insurgent knock
on the door of the unknown

A poem is its own Coney Island of
the mind
its own circus of the soul
its own Far Rockaway of the heart

Let a new lyricism
save the world
from itself